leap THROUGH TIME

Dinosaur

First published in the UK in 2002 by Chrysalis Children's Books,
an imprint of Chrysalis Books Group Plc
The Chrysalis Building, Bramley Road, London W10 6SP
www.chrysalisbooks.co.uk
This paperback edition first published in 2005

Senior Editor: Rasha Elsaeed

Created and produced by Nicholas Harris and Claire Aston,
Orpheus Books Ltd

Text Nicholas Harris

Illustrators pages 6-25 Peter David Scott (Wildlife Art Agency)
pages 26-29 Peter Dennis (Linda Rogers Associates)

Consultant Professor Michael Benton, Department of Earth Sciences,
University of Bristol, England

British Library Cataloguing in Publication Data for this book is available
from the British Library.

ISBN 1 901323 60 9 (hardback)
ISBN 1 84458 435 6 (paperback)

Printed and bound in Malaysia

leap THROUGH TIME

Dinosaur

illustrated by
Peter David Scott
text by
Nicholas Harris

CHRYSALIS CHILDREN'S BOOKS

Contents

Introduction

Imagine you are in China, many millions of years ago. All around you, there are hot, sticky forests and swamplands. The silence is shattered by shrieks and bellows as dinosaurs lumber across the landscape. Into this world is born a baby *Mamenchisaurus.* If he makes it to adulthood, he will grow into a 25-metre-long colossus. But dangers lurk everywhere, from the moment he hatches out. What will life hold in store for him?

The story told in this book is like a journey. It is not a journey from one place to another, but one in which you travel through time. With each turn of the page, the date moves forward a few days, a few years or many millions of years. Each time—every stop on your journey—is a new chapter in the life of the dinosaur. The early days in his mother's nest, the encounter with a pack of flesh-eaters, the journey to warmer lands with his own young family, his death and burial at the bottom of a river, the fossilization and later discovery of his remains—all tell the story of a dinosaur.

Look out for a tiny mammal. It lived in China at the same time as the Mamenchisaurus. It appears—in some form—in all of the illustrations.

Use this thumb index to travel through time! Just find the page you want to see and flip it open. This way you can make a quick comparison between one scene and another, even though some show events that took place some years apart. A little black arrow on the page points to the time of the scene illustrated on that page.

China, 160 million years ago

It is mid-morning, and already hot and humid. Dinosaurs of many different kinds are about. Their snorts and roars fill the air as they search for food. Two *Tuojiangosaurus*, dinosaurs with pointed plates running the length of their backs, plod around cropping ferns, while a *Shunosaurus* eats leaves from a tree, its spiked tail-club waving to and fro.

Mamenchisaurus

Shunosaurus

Tuojiangosaurus

Xiaosaurus

A group of tiny *Xiaosaurus* sprint away from the approaching flesh-eaters, *Yangchuanosaurus*, but two giant, long-necked *Mamenchisaurus* stand their ground. For now, the predators decide not to attack.

THE AGE OF DINOSAURS

The period from about 230 to 65 million years ago is called the Age of Dinosaurs. During that time, many different kinds of land-living, upright-walking reptiles spread to all parts of the world. Some were massive, lumbering plant-eaters, while others were fast-moving, two-legged hunters. Mammals also existed at this time, but they were all tiny, nocturnal creatures.

Shunosaurus

Tuojiangosaurus

Yangchuanosaurus

Pterosaur
(flying reptile)

7

A few weeks later ...

A group of *Mamenchisaurus* mothers have laid their eggs in clutches, each quite close to the others. To make their nests, they grub up the soil around the eggs using their teeth. The dinosaurs keep a watchful eye over their eggs. When a gang of small, fast-running, egg-eating dinosaurs launch a raid on the nests, a *Mamenchisaurus* swings her head low down to the ground and angrily chases them off, although not before a few eggs are grabbed.

DINOSAUR EGGS

Like many other reptiles and all modern birds, female dinosaurs laid eggs. The hard-shelled eggs were, in many cases, laid in nests made by scooping out bowl-shaped hollows in the soil or sand. For extra security, some dinosaurs made their nests together with others in breeding "colonies".

160 milli

A few v

9

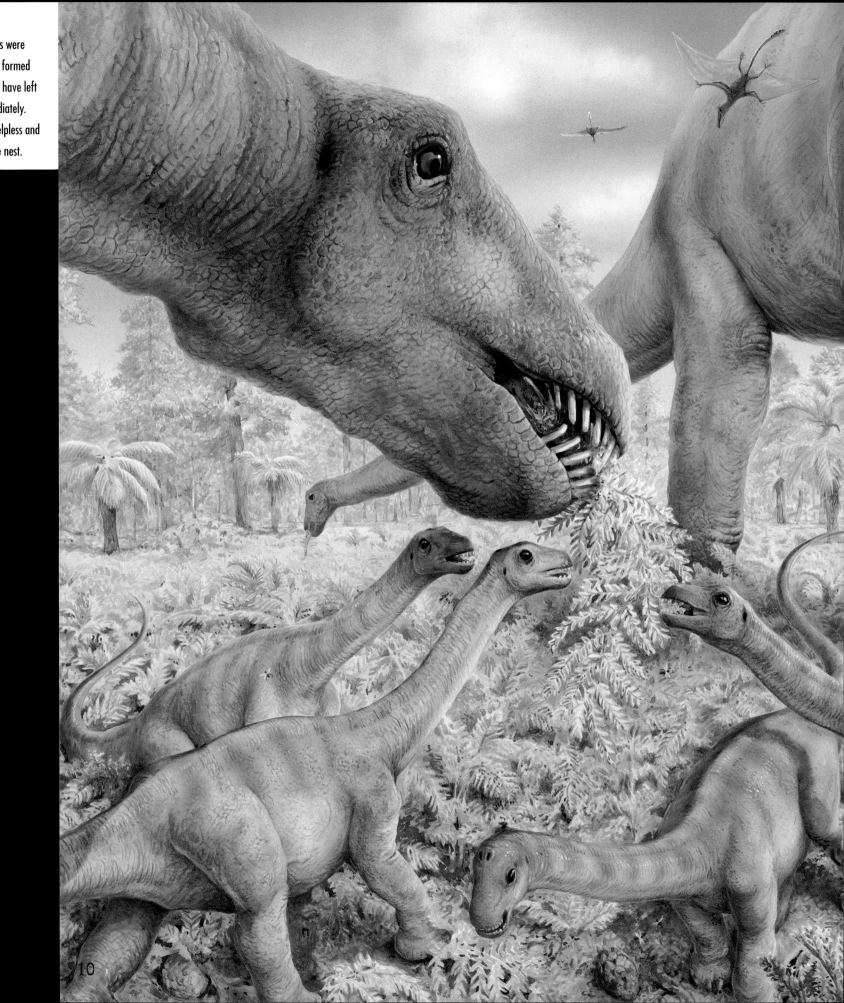

10

A few months later ...

The *Mamenchisaurus* young have hatched out. Compared to their parents, which measure up to 25 metres long, the hatchlings are tiny—about 40 centimetres soon after they are born. But they grow up quickly on a diet of ferns and other plants. Their parents crop ferns for them in their own mouths as the young dinosaurs have only tiny teeth.

The hatchlings are already quite adventurous. We shall follow the fortunes of one of them, whom we shall call Mamenchi (you can identify him by the colouring of his neck). His brother has to jump smartly out of the way when an adult fails to notice him as it lumbers past, nearly trampling him underfoot!

Despite being cared for by their parents, most of these young dinosaurs will fall prey to flesh-eating dinosaurs before they become adults themselves. They must remain on guard at all times. Only when they reach a length of about two metres or so will they be ready to roam further afield.

160 million years ago

A few weeks later

A few months later

FEEDING ON PLANTS

Mamenchisaurus was a sauropod, a large, plant-eating dinosaur with a long neck and tail and a small head. Sauropods used their long necks to browse on leaves that were high up in tall trees, low down on the ground or in the water. They needed to consume up to a tonne of vegetation per day. With only a row of thin teeth and no ability to chew their food, how did they manage to eat so much? They did so by swallowing pebbles, which helped to grind up their food into a thick paste in the gizzard (part of their stomachs), speeding up digestion.

A few years later ...

Mamenchi and his family are feeding from tree ferns at the edge of a forest. They use their immensely long necks (up to 15 metres long!) to reach high up to the treetops where the tenderest shoots are found. Both adults and young rear up on to their hind legs to gain an extra few metres of height.

While the dinosaurs concentrate on feeding, one of their number keeps a lookout for predators. Mamenchi, meanwhile, his appetite satisfied, gives himself a dust bath by rolling on the ground.

160 million years ago

A few weeks later

A few months later

A few years later

Some kinds of plant-eating dinosaurs were well-equipped to defend themselves. Spikes or clubs at the end of the tail were particularly effective when swung in the face of attackers.

A few minutes later ...

Suddenly a pack of *Yangchuanosaurus* burst on to the scene. The look-out bellows a warning, but the predators hurl themselves at the *Mamenchisaurus* herd. Their intended victims are the younger, smaller dinosaurs, but first they must tackle the adults. Mamenchi's parents rear up on their back legs and crash down on their attackers. They also flick their whip-like tails with great force in their faces. With the fighting at its fiercest, Mamenchi escapes unharmed.

FEEDING ON FLESH

Yangchuanosaurus was a theropod, the name given to all flesh-eating dinosaurs. Theropods ran on two muscular hind legs. Some, like *Tyrannosaurus rex*, were 12-metre-long giants, while the smallest were cat-sized. One group of small theropods were probably the ancestors of birds, and may have had feathers. A large flesh-eater killed or scavenged on its own, rushing at its victim and plunging its dagger-like teeth into its flesh. Smaller predators probably hunted in packs. This enabled them to bring down victims much larger than themselves.

160 million years ago

A few weeks later

A few months later

A few years later

A few minutes later

15

There were two groups of dinosaurs: ornithischians, which had backward-sloping pubic bones (1) and saurischians, with forward-jutting ones (2). *Mamenchisaurus*, a sauropod, was a saurischian.

A few years later ...

Mamenchi has grown into an adult and now has a family of his own. His family belong to a much larger herd of dinosaurs. They all stay together for protection against predators.

As winter sets in and the vegetation dies back, the herd sets out for richer forests and swamplands hundreds of kilometres to the south. The long winter days and lower temperatures signal to the dinosaurs that the time has come. They cannot survive cold conditions.

The young walk in the centre of the migrating herd, while some adult *Mamenchisaurus* keep a lookout for danger. They know that predatory dinosaurs will stealthily accompany the herd, watching for stragglers, as it marches southwards.

DINOSAUR HERDS

Like some plant-eating animals today, many plant-eating dinosaurs lived in herds. Fossil finds show members of the same group of dinosaurs, young and old, living (and dying) close together. By being part of a herd, the individual dinosaurs found extra protection in numbers. Some male members of the herd would have fought each other to be its leader. A well-ordered group with a powerful leader would have been more likely to resist an attack.

160 million years ago

A few weeks later

A few months later

A few years later

A few minutes later

A few years later

Fossils can tell us a great deal about how dinosaurs lived—and died. A very unusual fossil was found in Mongolia in 1971. It is of two dinosaurs, a *Velociraptor* and a *Protoceratops,* locked in deadly combat. The *Velociraptor,* a small, two-legged predator, is grasping the head of the *Protoceratops,* while the hooked claws on its feet prepare to gash the belly of its unfortunate victim.

FLASH FLOOD

Not even the largest dinosaurs could survive nature's most powerful forces. Sudden heavy rain could lead to flash floods. Water surged down a steep gully (a channel that is normally dry) destroying all in its path.

A few weeks later ...

On their journey south, the herd have to cross a ravine. As Mamenchi and others wade across, there is a sudden flood. The shallow, slow-flowing water rapidly becomes a deep, raging torrent. Some of the dinosaurs manage to clamber out the other side. But Mamenchi has stayed in the water to help other family members across. He loses his footing and is swept away by the great force of the current...

160 million years ago

A few weeks later

A few months later

A few years later

A few minutes later

A few years later

A few weeks later

Ten years later ...

Mamenchi never escaped from the flood. The giant dinosaur soon drowned. His body slumped to the bottom of the river, where it was immediately covered over by mud and silt swept along by the swirling torrent. Soon, the river became calm again. Months later, all the soft parts of the dinosaur's body, the skin, flesh and organs, have rotted away, leaving only the hard parts, the teeth and bones. The bones are so heavy, even strong currents cannot shift them.

Batrachognathus (pterosaurs)

Tuojiangosaurus

Turtle

While Mamenchi's remains lie beneath the river bed, life goes on. As dinosaurs come to the river's edge to drink, pterosaurs (flying reptiles) flit back and forth looking for fish to pluck from the water's surface. In the water, fish and turtles seek out their prey.

PRESERVED IN STONE (1)

For a dinosaur to die in this way was a stroke of luck for scientists today. The conditions were perfect for the formation of fossils. If a living thing were quickly cloaked by sediments (sand, gravel, mud and other rock fragments), oxygen would be kept out. This meant that bacteria, which cause decay, could not survive. The creature's bones were preserved long enough for the process of fossilization to begin.

160 million years ago

A few weeks later

A few months later

A few years later

A few minutes later

A few years later

A few weeks later

Ten years later

Huanhepterus (pterosaurs)

Aspidorhynchus

Mamenchi's skeleton

All the dinosaurs died out at the end of the Cretaceous Period, 65 million years ago. The extinction was quite abrupt. Scientists think that either a massive asteroid (a large rocky object in space) crashed to Earth *(above)* or that there was a huge volcanic eruption *(below)*. Both events would have filled the atmosphere with dust, blotting out the Sun for many years.

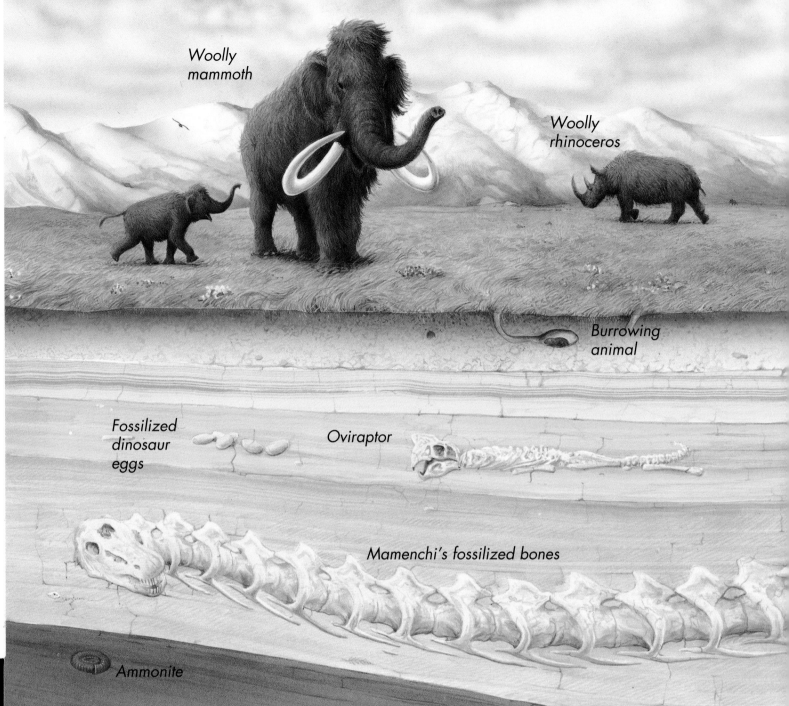

Woolly mammoth

Woolly rhinoceros

Burrowing animal

Fossilized dinosaur eggs

Oviraptor

Mamenchi's fossilized bones

Ammonite

Millions of years later ...

Mamenchi's remains have turned to stone. Over many years, more and more sediments collected at the bottom of the river. The tiny rock fragments were gradually pressed together to form new rocks. As millions of years passed, more layers of sediments, more layers of rock and more animals' remains all built up.

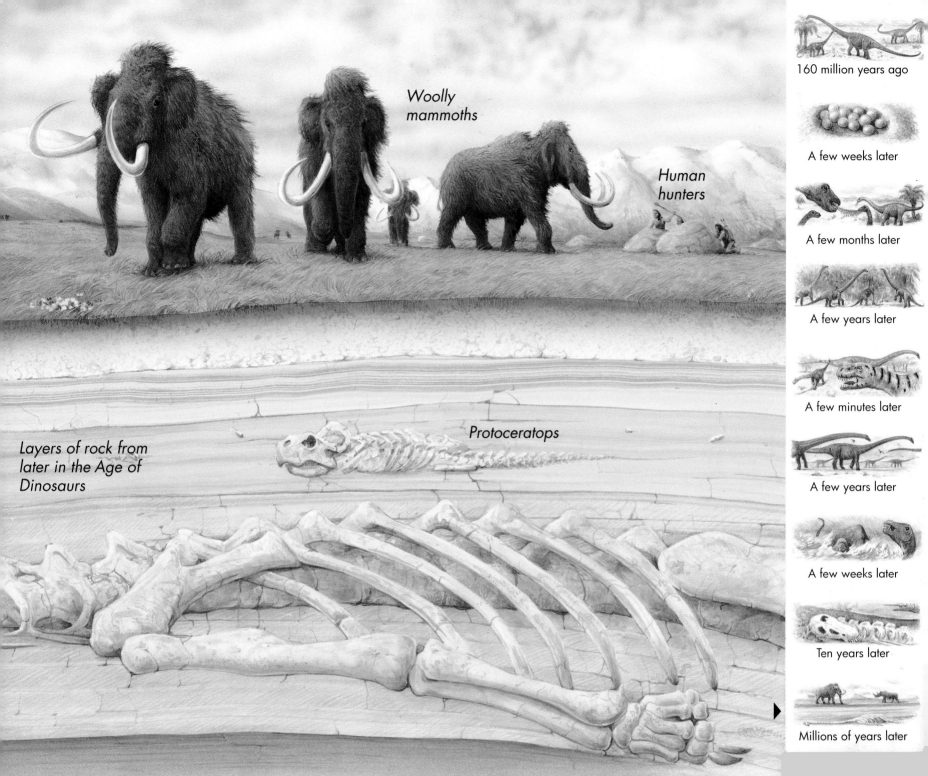

Woolly mammoths

Human hunters

Layers of rock from later in the Age of Dinosaurs

Protoceratops

160 million years ago

A few weeks later

A few months later

A few years later

A few minutes later

A few years later

A few weeks later

Ten years later

Millions of years later

Now it is the Ice Ages, a time in the story of the Earth when the climate was cooler and winters were long. Woolly mammoths and rhinoceroses (and people who hunt them) roam the grassy plains.

PRESERVED IN STONE (2)

As the sediments lying above a skeleton turned to rock, water, with minerals dissolved in it, seeped into pores (tiny holes) in the bones. Gradually the bone material was completely replaced by the minerals and became part of the surrounding rock—while preserving the exact shape of the original bones.

Over the 165 million years' span of the Age of Dinosaurs, the Earth changed. The great land masses, or continents, moved about the surface of the globe. The Earth's outer shell is divided up into large slabs, called tectonic plates, that slowly slide around, their edges grinding against each other. In the Jurassic Period (when *Mamenchisaurus* lived), the continents were packed closely together *(above)*. They drifted apart in the Cretaceous Period *(below)*.

Eighteen thousand years later ...

The bitterly cold years of the Ice Ages are over. Mammoths have long died out. Now it is people who rule the Earth.

It so happens that on this spot, just where Mamenchi fell millions of years ago, the upper layers of soil and rock have crumbled away. Two children, playing nearby, notice what looks like bones of a huge animal in the ground ...

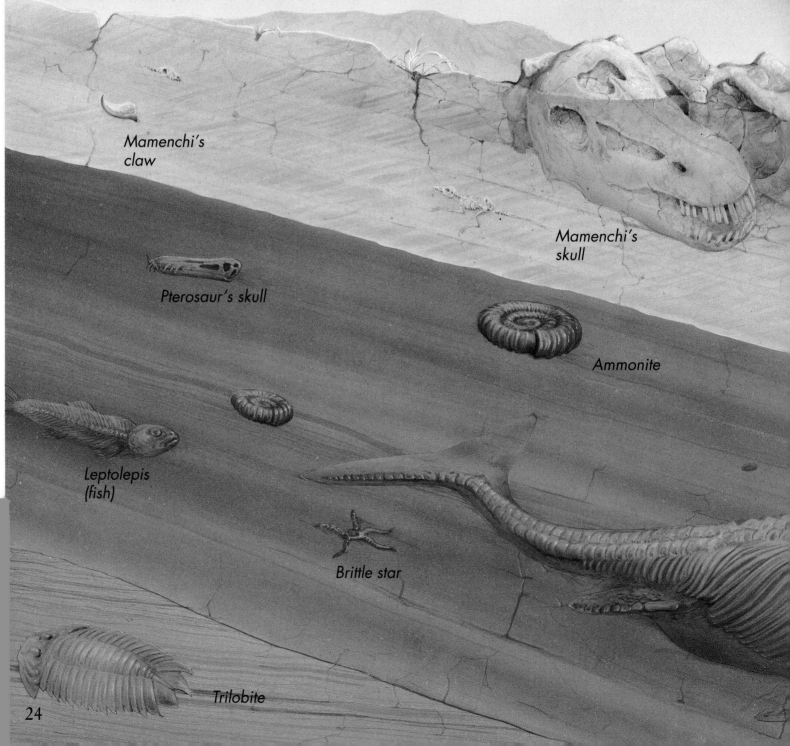

Mamenchi's claw

Pterosaur's skull

Mamenchi's skull

Ammonite

Leptolepis (fish)

Brittle star

Trilobite

PRESERVED IN STONE (3)

Over millions of years, many layers of sediment were built up, both during the later part of the Age of Dinosaurs, and ever since. Living things were fossilized in the rocks of their time. So looking at a slice through the rocks is like reading a story of prehistoric life. Earth movements over time have, in many places, pushed up or squashed some layers of rock, bringing some fossils back to the surface.

160 million years ago

A few weeks later

A few months later

A few years later

A few minutes later

A few years later

A few weeks later

Ten years later

Millions of years later

A few years ago

Mamenchi's neck bones

Ichthyosaur

25

Palaeontologists use a number of different tools to free fossils from the surrounding rock, or matrix. These include hammers, picks, drills, needles and brushes.

"Sue" is a near-complete *Tyrannosaurus rex* fossil discovered in 1990. Its skull, scarred and slightly squashed, is 1.5 metres long and weighs 340 kilograms.

Bones and teeth are not the only fossil finds we have of the dinosaurs. Footprints are examples of trace fossils. They can indicate the size, weight and speed of a dinosaur.

A few months later ...

The children rushed home to tell their parents of their amazing discovery. Scientists from the Natural History Museum were contacted. They sent a team of experts to inspect the find. They were very excited about what they saw—a rare example of a *Mamenchisaurus* skeleton! An excavation was organized straight away.

Now a team of scientists called palaeontologists, who specialize in the study of fossils, are carefully digging into the rock all around the bones that the children found. Using picks and shovels, as well as thin blades and even toothbrushes, they remove some of the surrounding rock from the fossilized skeleton. The palaeontologists number all the bones, record their exact positions and photograph them. They paint a sticky substance called resin on the bones to stop them crumbling. Then they carefully place the bones in sacks packed with plastic foam, and send them off to the museum.

Clearing rubble

Skull

Working on laptop computer

Discoverers of Mamenchi's fossil skeleton

Photographer

Shoulder bone

Palaeontologists remove rock from fossil

Recording details

Painting resin

160 million years ago

A few weeks later

A few months later

A few years later

A few minutes later

A few years later

A few weeks later

Ten years later

Millions of years later

A few years ago

A few months later

27

There were hundreds of kinds of dinosaur, from all over the world and living in different times. Visit your nearest museum to see the skeletons of just a few of them. Below are artists' drawings of how some dinosaurs may have looked when alive.

Parasaurolophus had a hollow, backward-pointing crest. This may have acted like a megaphone, boosting its call.

Saichania's body was covered with bony studs and spikes. It also had a bony club on its tail.

Oviraptor had a strange, parrot-shaped head. It may have fed on eggs.

Baryonyx may have used its curved thumb-claws to catch fish.

Today, six years later ...

Having lain undisturbed in his rocky tomb for more than 100 million years, Mamenchi once again stands proudly on his four mighty limbs! In a painstaking task, the museum staff have expertly put Mamenchi's skeleton back together again. Using steel rods and cables, they have mounted it in pride of place in the museum's main exhibition area. Visitors who have come from far afield flock to see this new wonder, and stare in amazement at its great size.

Mamenchi's skeleton

Shunosaurus

Discoverers of Mamenchi's fossil skeleton

CD-rom of Mamenchi's life

The guides are on hand to tell the visitors more about the dinosaur, along with the other creatures that shared his world. The children who discovered it a few years ago are frequent visitors to the museum. But only you, the reader, know Mamenchi's full story ...

THE MUSEUM LABORATORY

The fossil dinosaur is prepared for display in the museum laboratory. The work goes on to remove any remaining rock. Instruments such as dental drills take out the smallest fragments. Close study of the bones, including computer scans of inside the skull, enable scientists to find out, for example, what the dinosaur fed on or how intelligent it was.

160 million years ago

A few weeks later

A few months later

A few years later

A few minutes later

A few years later

A few weeks later

Ten years later

Millions of years later

A few years ago

A few months later

Today

Pterosaur

Yangchuanosaurus

Glossary

Bacteria Tiny organisms made up of only one cell. They can be seen only through a powerful microscope. They are not members of either the plant or animal kingdoms, and have their own separate kingdom. Bacteria play a vital role in recycling nutrients in nature.

Continental drift The movement of continents (the Earth's great land masses) around the globe. The Earth's outer layer is made up of separate tectonic plates, which are constantly on the move, pushing into, pulling away from or sliding alongside one another, taking continents or parts of continents with them.

Dinosaurs Reptiles that lived on land during the Mesozoic Era (250-65 million years ago). Dinosaurs walked upright on legs held beneath their bodies, as do birds and mammals today. Flying reptiles and marine reptiles were *not* dinosaurs.

Fossils The ancient remains or traces of once-living things, usually found preserved in rock. A living thing becomes fossilized when it is buried by sediments and the tiny spaces inside its hard parts are filled with minerals which set hard over time.

Ice Ages A cold period in the Earth's history when ice spread out from the poles and mountain ranges to cover large areas of the Earth's surface. The last Ice Age began about 2 million years ago and may not have ended yet.

Matrix The surrounding rock in which a fossil is embedded.

Minerals Natural chemical substances that are neither plant nor animal. Rocks are made up of minerals. Minerals are the commonest solid material found on the Earth.

Ornithischians The "bird-hipped" dinosaurs, one of two major types of dinosaur (the other is saurischian). Ornithischians had backward-sloping pubic bones—the lower part of the hip bone.

Palaeontologists Scientists who study fossils.

Predators Animals that prey on others.

Pterosaurs Flying reptiles that existed from the late Triassic to late Cretaceous Periods. Their wings were formed from skin flaps between the fourth finger and lower body.

Saurischians The "lizard-hipped" dinosaurs, one of two major types of dinosaur (the other is ornithischian). Saurischians had forward-jutting pubic bones—the lower part of the hip bone.

Sauropods Long-necked, four-legged, plant-eating dinosaurs. They were the very largest and heaviest land animals of all time.

Sediments Eroded rock fragments that are transported by wind, water or ice and laid down elsewhere.

Tectonic plates The large slabs into which the entire Earth's surface is divided. The plates, 15 in all, move relative to one another around the globe.

Theropods All the meat-eating saurischian dinosaurs.

Index